Watch Me BLOOM

For my dear friends Thuc Chinh, Stuart and Elliott.
"Blossoming moments, beautifully constant."

Krina Patel-Sage

Lantana

Snowdrop

Pushing up through snow, these delicate flowers are stronger than they look.

Rose

Sweet red Valentine's,
each petal a reminder
of how much you're loved.

Daffodil

Bright, happy trumpets
call in golden sunshine to
cheer up rainy days.

Bluebell

Fairy umbrellas
crowded together in a
woodland sea of blue.

Cherry blossom

Pink flower clouds burst!
Petals gently fall like a
joyful springtime gift.

Daisy

Crowning each other
with white-studded chains. What fun
on sunny picnics!

Buttercup

Little yellow chins
follow that age-old question:
do you like butter?

Azalea

Fiery petals
in lucky red: dragon flames
from granny's childhood.

Dandelion

Yellow-maned flowers
turn into tempting puffballs,
waiting to float free.

Cornflower

Carefree fields of blue
are made for laughing, dancing
and twirling with joy!

Cosmos

Perfectly-arranged
petals; nature's harmony
is all around us.

Lavender

Sweet-smelling blossoms
loved by bees and butterflies.
Breathe in peaceful calm.

Lotus

Rising with the sun,
graceful blooms close at nightfall,
sinking down to sleep.

Night blooming water lily

Pretty water stars
open to catch bright moonbeams
glowing through the night.

Borage

Planted side-by-side,
garden stars make perfect friends,
helping others grow.

Foxglove

Little bee pockets,
just right for hide and seek or
games of peekaboo!

Poppy

Vibrant pops of red
turn up where least expected,
bold, fearless and strong.

Gladiolus

Magnificent blooms
decorate city windows,
cheering passers-by.

Hollyhock

From tall, sturdy stems
showy faces look outward,
proud and confident.

Sunflower

Towering beacons
burn bright in summer gardens.
It's my time to shine!

Fuchsia

Tropical jewels

in brightest pink and purple:

Grandpa's pride and joy.

Marigold

Beaming orange suns
bring light to happy couples
on their wedding day.

Orchid

This beautiful gift
will bloom again and again
if handled with care.

Poinsettia

Tiny white flowers
surrounded by flame-red leaves,
bringing festive warmth.

Floral Fun Facts

Young sunflowers track the sun. They start off facing east and move their heads towards the west throughout the day.

Poppies can grow in unlikely places. They can even sprout from cracks in the concrete where small amounts of soil have collected.

The poinsettia originates from Mexico and Central America where it is known as "Christmas Eve flower." Aztecs used it for red dye and medicine.

Lotus flowers rise up and open in the daytime. They slowly close as darkness falls, sinking back into the water. Their seeds can stay at the bottom of a pond for many years. The oldest seeds known to sprout were 1,300 years old!

Borage, also known as "starflower," helps certain plants to grow by repelling harmful insects and attracting helpful pollinators like bees and butterflies.

Snowdrops flower in cold weather. They have been known to pop up through layers of snow!

Cherry blossoms bloom for only a short time. They are celebrated in a Japanese festival called "Hanami," meaning "flower viewing."

Marigolds are used in Hindu weddings and festivals. They represent the sun and its positive energy.

In Mexico, marigolds are used in Day of the Dead celebrations to help guide spirits home.

The word "cosmos" comes from the Greek "kosmos," meaning "world order." Spanish priests named the flower for its evenly-spaced petals, reflecting a harmonius universe.

Bluebells poking up through soil in spring are a sign of ancient woodland. Thousands of flowers bloom all at once to form a bright violet-blue "carpet" on the woodland floor.

In China, the azalea is known as "thinking of home bush."

Gladioli get their name from the Latin word "gladius," meaning "sword," due to the shape of their long pointy leaves.

Each entry in this book highlights one or more of the "Five Ways to Wellbeing," shown below. These are steps that have been proven to boost mental health, increase positivity and help us get the best out of life.

Connect   **Be Active**   **Take Notice**   **Keep Learning**   **Give**

Huge thanks to super cool Theo Williams for inspiring the cover character.

First published in the United Kingdom in 2023 by Lantana Publishing Ltd.
Clavier House, 21 Fifth Road, Newbury RG14 6DN, UK
www.lantanapublishing.com | info@lantanapublishing.com

American edition published in 2023 by Lantana Publishing Ltd., UK.

Distributed in the United States and Canada by Lerner Publishing Group, Inc.
241 First Avenue North, Minneapolis, MN 55401 U.S.A.
For reading levels and more information, look for this title at www.lernerbooks.com
Cataloging-in-Publication Data Available.

Hardback ISBN: 978-1-913747-99-2
PDF ISBN: 978-1-911373-93-3
ePub3 ISBN: 978-1-915244-44-4

Printed and bound in China using sustainably sourced paper and plant-based inks.
Original artwork created digitally.